Skylite and Bumpy's Rocking Chair

PATTY HAMILL

PAGE PUBLISHING
Conneaut Lake, PA

First originally published by Page Publishing 2022

ISBN 978-1-6624-8609-8 (pbk)
ISBN 978-1-6624-8618-0 (hc)
ISBN 978-1-6624-8612-8 (digital)

Printed in the United States of America

I want to dedicate this book to two very special people in my life. One is Derrick who made me believe in myself and to keep my dream alive. This man came into my life and took Skylites Adventure internationally. Now, with this new book Skylite and Bumpies Rocking Chair is I think my best one so does Derrick and my sister Sandi.

To my sister Sandi, who listened to me read my story over and over without saying a word.

It was all good feedback and the laughter we shared with this book is something I will never forget.

Love you both

Dozzie was whistling on his way to visit Skylite.

Suddenly Dozzie found himself knocked to the ground. Stunned, Dozzie yelled, "Skylite, what are you doing and why did you knock me down?"

Gasping for breath, Skylite anxiously spoke, "I need your help. Sorry I knocked you over. I just could not stop. This new thing I discovered I could fly is so thrilling!"

"Never mind that," Skylite spoke. "Dozzie, so you found me. What do you want?"

Skylite was darting all around. Dozzie said, "I need your help. We need to get back to Timber-Stick Town now. I need every stick to help me!"

"What is going on you frantic little bug?"

"Well, you see, Dozzie, I was flying all over in the field, and I saw this turkey limping, so I flew by him and noticed how hurt he was. We need to help him," spoke Skylite.

"But, Skylite, they eat bugs like us," said Dozzie.

"I know," spoke Skylite, "but he needs our help."

"But how?" asked Dozzie

"Dozzie, can you help me?" asked Skylite. "I have an idea that might work"

As Dozzie and Skylite entered Timber-Stick Town, to their surprise all the sticks were jumping with so much joy and yelling "OUR HERO, SKYLITE!"

Dozzie standing on a limb. "We need to help, Skylite!"

"Help with what?" Skylite asked.

I found a turkey that was hurt, and I want to help him!

"OH NO!" gasped the sticks. "Skylite, they eat us! I am not ready to be a meal for him. No one is! And you, Skylite. Turkeys eat you also!"

"PLEASE," begged Skylite, "I will protect you I PROMISE!"

The sticks thought about it and then they all agreed to help. After saying goodbye to their families and BeBees splinters they left for their journey.

Skylite flew ahead to find the turkey. As he came upon the turkey, Skylite wanting to help was attacked.

Skylite, "WHOA, I came to help you! What is your name?" asked Skylite.

The turkey replied, "Go away, and leave me alone. I am hungry and hurt. Go away or I will eat you!"

Skylite yelled, "NO! I came to help you!"

"What?" replied the turkey, "To help me?"

"Yes, my friends are here to help find a safe place before the storm starts. Look! Over there Mr. and Mrs. Barktree are holding my friends, the walking sticks."

"You all came to help me?" the turkey spoke as he sobbed.

"What is your name?" asked Skylite.

"BUMPY," spoke the turkey!

"Bumpy. Oh, that is a nice name for a turkey! It is better than TOM."

"What happened?"

Bumpy responded with tears in his eyes, "ZAPPO and his zappions. They started to chase me, and I could not fly that well and I tripped and hurt my leg."

Gasping, Skylite said, "OH NO, NOT ZAPPO AGAIN!"

"Yes," Bumpy replied while crying.

"Well, don't you worry Bumpy we are here to help you all of us!"

"WOW," Bumpy sobbed. "Thank you so much."

"You stay here, Bumpy, until I find a place that is safe for you, and I will bring some food to you," said Skylite.

Bumpy asked, "Skylite? Are you the same Skylite that saved the Princess of Neon?"

"Why, yes," spoke Skylite.

"So, you really are the hero everyone talks about! wow," said Bumpy

Skylite flew over to Dozzie and the walking sticks. Skylite asked Dozzie if they found a spot yet and Dozzie replied, "yes. Oh, Skylite you are going to be so happy."

"well, tell me," said Skylite. "It is a cave and big enough for the turkey? By the way, what is the turkey's name?" asked Dozzie

"His name is Bumpy!" replied Skylite.

'Hey, Skylite, better than another tom," laughed Dozzie.

"Can Bumpy make it to the cave?" Skylite asked.

"No."

"Great, so how do we get Bumpy to safety?"

Bumpy spoke up and said, "A sling?"

"How?" asked Skylite and Dozzie.

"Let's start by lining up on both sides of me for the length."

Dozzie spoke, "Well, let's go. Bumpy will not eat us. All the walking sticks lined up on either side of Bumpy," and Dozzie spoke up, "I got it. It's so simple. We can hang onto one another from side to side. This will give Bumpy a place to lay down while we move him!"

"YEAH!" all the sticks are so happy to be able to help Bumpy.

As Bumpy moved closer to get on the sling, everyone went screaming and running to Mr. and Mrs. Barktree. IT was Zappo and his zapping. Skylite flew up immediately and stopped Zappo.

He yelled at Zappo, "What do you want?"

"Well, Skylite. I feel so bad for what I did, and I would like to help you all."

Skylite said, "HMMMMMM, can we trust you?"

"YES, oh please, give me a chance. I promise I will be good from now on. I am tired of being a bad bug."

"This is your last chance, Zappo," said Skylite. "Okay, let's start all over again."

Z
Z
Z

"Yes," spoke Zappo. Zappo and his zappions also helped in lining up the sticks for Bumpy.

"Bumpy, can you get on the sling?" asked Dozzie and Skylite.

"I will try," said Bumpy. Bumpy could not move. "oh, no!" cried Bumpy. "What now?"

Zappo spoke up, "I and my zappions can lift you onto the sling."

They went to either side of Bumpy and started to lift him. "wow!" exclaimed Bumpy. "I am on the sling." Skylite and Dozzie went to Bumpy. "Are you ready?

"Why yes," spoke Bumpy.

"Hang on. Here we go."

Moving toward the cave Zappo noticed something. He was flashing, and it was getting darker and windier. He was guiding everyone to the cave. Skylite was so surprised Zappo lit up and was flashing.

"How can I and my zappions flash?" he asked.

"Simple," said Skylite. "Because you are doing good by helping someone in need of help."

Upon entering the cave, the rain started. "Just in time," spoke up Skylite. "Now we need something for Bumpy to sit on."

"I got it, Skylite," said Dozzie. "If we can build a sling, we can build a rocking chair!"

"A rocking chair?"

"Why yes!"

All the walking sticks built a rocking chair for Bumpy. Bumpy was so tearful and grateful that the food he eats saved him from harm. "Wow," said Bumpy. "Thank you, all. I thought I was going to die, but you all saved me!"

Zappo and his Zappions were flashing and flying all around. Zappo spoke to everyone and said, "I promise, Skylite. I will take good care of Bumpy until he is well, and I will take care of all the walking sticks that built the sling and chair."

About the Author

Patty just moved from Maine to California to be with her future husband, Derrick, and yes, she never expected to make such a move… best decision! Since she wrote the first book a lot has changed in her life. Skylite's Adventure went international, and it has been a big hit. Since then, Patty wrote her second book as part of Skylite's Adventure. She had fun writing her first book, BUT this book is a lot of fun. Will Patty continue with the series of Skylite's Adventure? Maybe. He is her hero of the forests.